LOOK AT

HOMES, HOLES, AND HIVES

Franklin Watts
387 Park Avenue South
New York
N.Y. 10016

Library of Congress Cataloging-in-Publication Data
Pluckrose, Henry Arthur.
Homes, holes, and hives / Henry Pluckrose.
p. cm. — (Look at)
Summary: Examines different animal homes, how they are constructed, and how they are adapted to suit the life of each animal.
ISBN 0-531-14046-6
1. Animals—Habitations—Juvenile literature. [1. Animals—
—Habitations.] I. Title.
QL756.P56 1990 90-12178
591.56′4—dc20 CIP AC

Editor: Kate Petty
Design Concept: David Bennett

Phototypeset by Lineage Ltd, Watford
Printed in Italy by G. Canale & C.S.p.A. – Turin

Photographs: B and C Alexander 6t; H Angel 8t; Biofotos 24r, 26; Bruce Coleman 18t, 18b; Chris Fairclough Colour Library 4r, 23l, 28, 29r; Hutchison Library 6b; Natural History Photographic Agency 11t, 15r, 24l, 24c, 27l; Oxford Scientific Films 8b, 17r; Planet Earth Pictures 11b, 13; Survival Anglia 9tl, 9b, 10t, 10b, 12bl, 14, 15l, 16, 17l, 19t, 20r, 21, 22, 23r, 25t, 27r, 29l; ZEFA 4l, 4b, 5t, 5b, 7, 9c, 12t, 19b, 20l, 25br.

Front cover: Oxford Scientific Films

LOOK AT

HOMES, HOLES, AND HIVES

Henry Pluckrose

FRANKLIN WATTS

New York • London • Sydney • Toronto

Most human beings have some kind of home. They need a home to protect them from the weather and as a place to bring up children. Some live in cities, in appartments, and houses.

Some live in cottages.

Not all homes are built of stone and brick.
These homes are made of mud and thatch.

Some people live a wandering life.
Samit (Lapps) follow their reindeer.

Bedouin people travel across the desert
with their camels...

...and some people seem to prefer
a home on wheels.

The spider spins a silken web.
Her ‘home’ is also a trap for insects.

The bumble bee lines her nest
with silk mixed with pollen.

Wild honey bees build a nest in the trees. Domestic honey bees are kept in a hive. Wherever they are, the worker bees build wax chambers in which the queen bee lays her eggs.

Tiny termites build a huge mound that may be over nine feet high.
They stick the earth together with their own saliva. Inside the mound are many passages lined with little scraps of wood.

The Nile crocodile protects the eggs in her nest by covering it with mud. She hears the babies chirping when they are ready to hatch, and digs them out.

Moles dig long tunnels through the earth.
In springtime, some of these tunnels are turned into nesting chambers.
The network of tunnels is called a "fortress."

The wombat is a burrowing mammal that lives in Australia. It is a marsupial, like the koala and the kangaroo, and carries its baby in a pouch.

The fox's underground home is called a "burrow."

Rabbits live together in large groups.
Their underground home is called a "warren."

Leverets

The hare lives alone. The mother makes a shallow nest, called a "form."
Baby hares are "leverets."

Many rodents (animals that gnaw) spend part of their lives underground. Water voles live in burrows along the banks of streams.

The house mouse lives in holes and cracks in walls and floors.

The harvest mouse builds a nest above ground. She weaves a round house from grasses.

North American Woodchuck

Black bear

When winter comes, some animals move underground to hibernate. They sleep through the worst of the cold weather. The North American Woodchuck hibernates in a burrow or a hollow log.

In the autumn, the female polar bear makes a den in the snow. She has her cubs there in the middle of winter.
They dig themselves out when it is spring.

North American beavers work hard to build their "lodge." They dam a stream with logs and branches to make a pond. They tunnel into the bank to make a living chamber.

Some creatures that live near water do not bother to build a nest. Seals spend most of their time in the sea. Their pups are born on land in rocky hollows.

Penguins make rough nests of grass and weeds in gaps between rocks. They nest very closely together in "rookeries." This makes it difficult for a predator to steal an egg or a chick.

Most water birds nest close to the water's edge, like this grebe.

A swan becomes very angry if an intruder comes into her nesting area.

Birds that live in hedges build nests with twigs, grass, earth and moss. The African weaver bird weaves its roosting platform amongst the reeds.

Song thrush

Treecreeper

African weaver bird

Woodland birds often nest in holes in trees.

The golden eagle lives in wild, rocky places.
Its nest is built on a rock face where
there is space to raise the eaglets.
The eagles' home is called an "aerie."

The stork also needs space to nest!

Bats are mammals that fly.
Most bats hunt and feed when it is dark.
They spend the hours of daylight hanging upsidedown in caves and in the rafters of old buildings.

Chimpanzees make nests in the trees to sleep in, but most apes and monkeys do not build homes or nests.
The olive baboon sleeps in the trees.
It feeds on the land around the trees.

Wildebeest

Animals that graze have no fixed home.
They wander in search of food.
Their babies need to be able to get up
and walk as soon as they are born.

Some creatures are always at home.
The snail's shell protects its soft body.

The tortoise is also safe from enemies.
It can retreat right into its shell.

Did you know?

● The stickleback is one of the few fishes that build a home. The male stickleback builds a nest of roots and stalks, which it sticks together with a paste. The paste is made by the stickleback. Eggs are then laid in the nest by the female. The male fish guards the eggs.

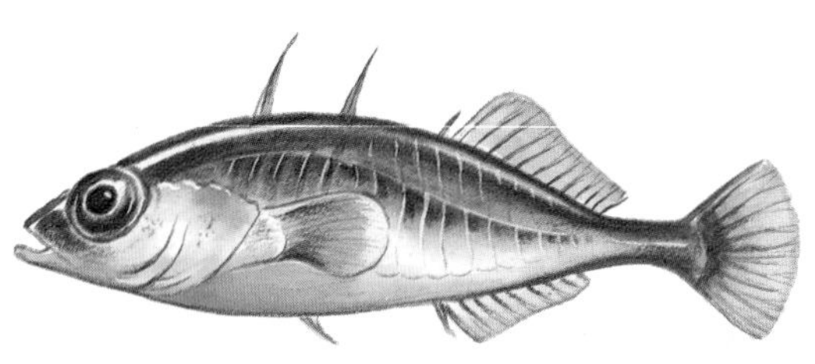

● The hedgehog finds it difficult to make a burrow. When it is ready to hibernate for the winter, it finds a hollow out of the wind, snuggles down into a bed of leaves, and rolls up into a tight ball to sleep.

● Some birds, like the golden-backed weaver, choose trees near water for nesting. They select a branch overhanging a river or a lake. The water below gives extra protection to the eggs and chicks in the nest.

Something to try

● Collect some twigs, moss, and a little clay. Try to build a nest in the branches of a bush or a small tree. You will find it very difficult! When a bird builds a nest it has to carry each piece of material to the nest site – and its "tools" are two feet and a beak.

Which animals live in groups called...?

a charm
a colony
a flock
a gaggle
a herd
a leap
a pack
a pride
a swarm
a troop

Sayings

To be taken under someone's wing
To have a nest egg
To feather one's nest

Can you find out...?

- Who had a nest built in his beard by two owls, a hen, four larks and a wren?

Words about houses and homes

aerie
burrow
cave
cover
den
earth
form
haunt
hive
hole
home
lair
nest
perch
roost
set
territory
warren

What creatures might you find in...?

an apiary
an aviary
an earth
a hatchery
a heronry
a hill

Index